Illustrations by b.m. king

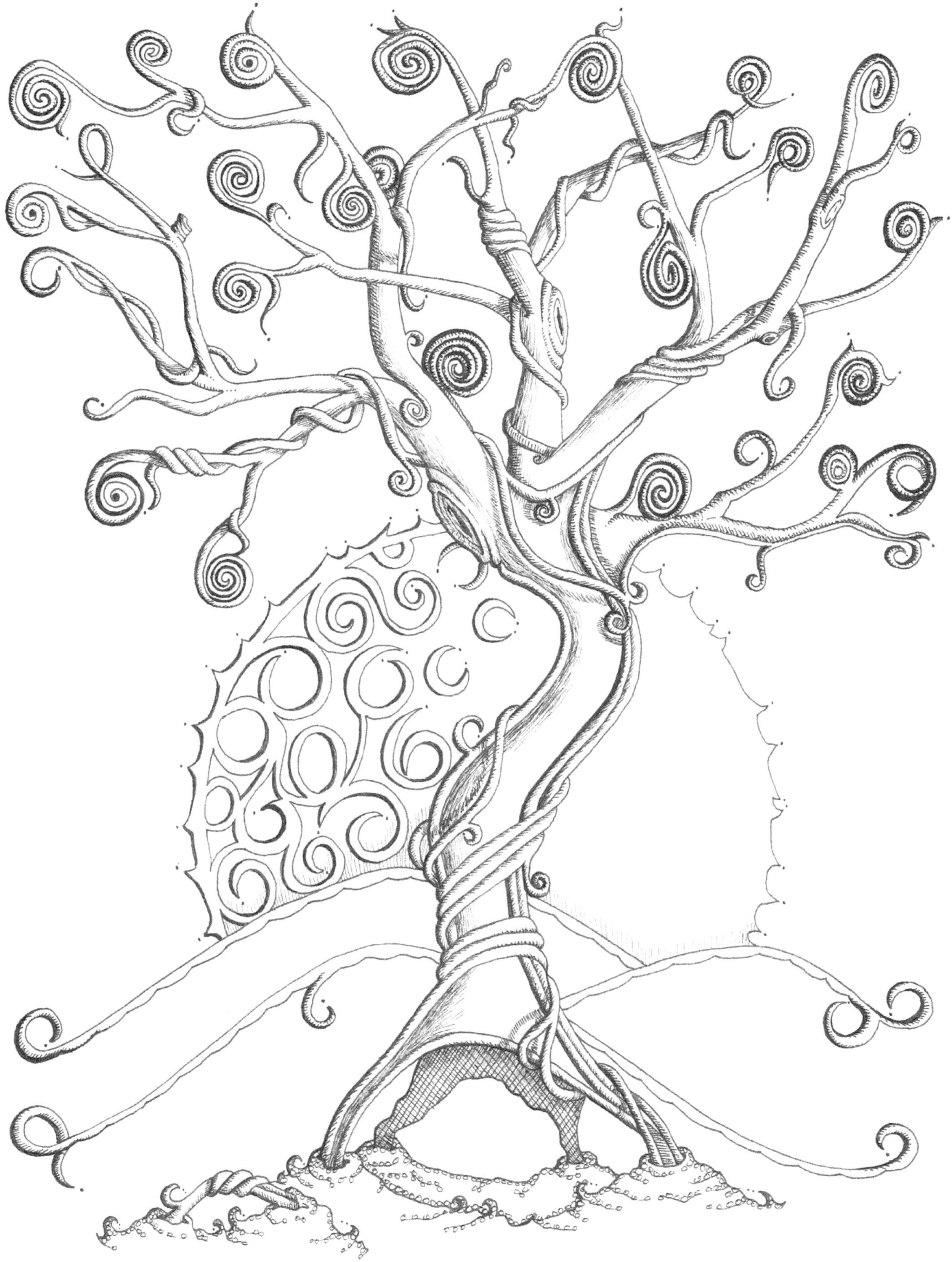

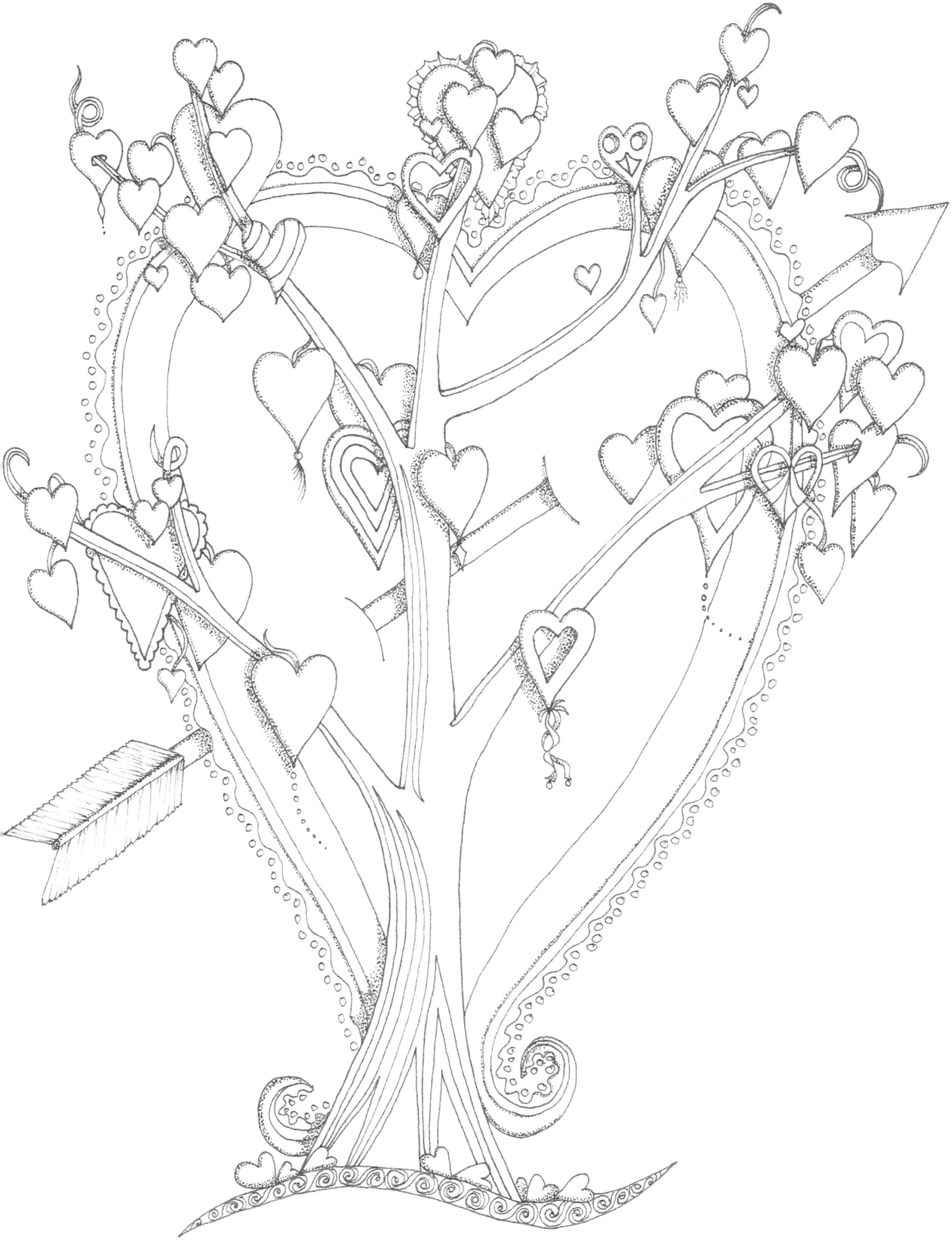

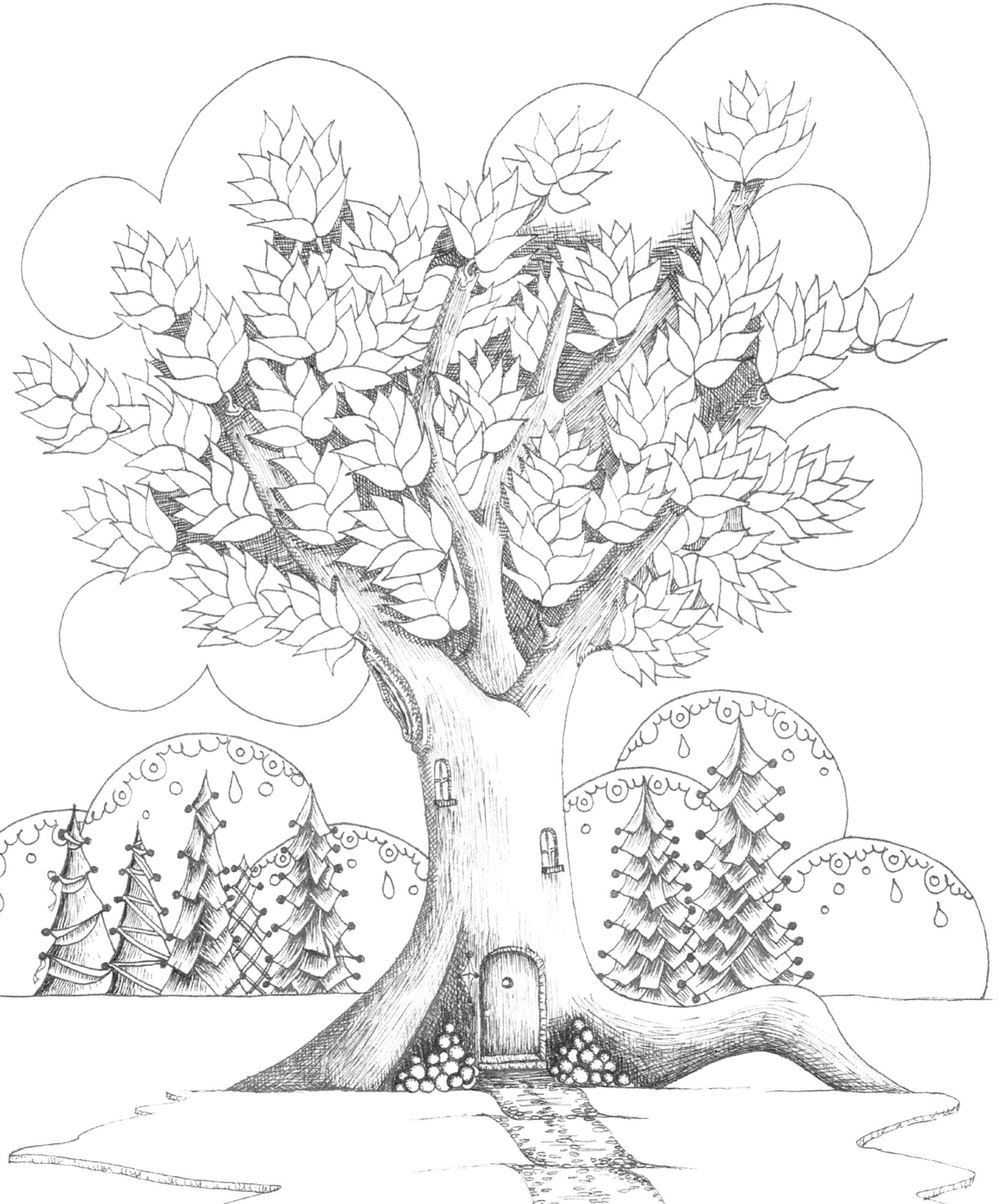

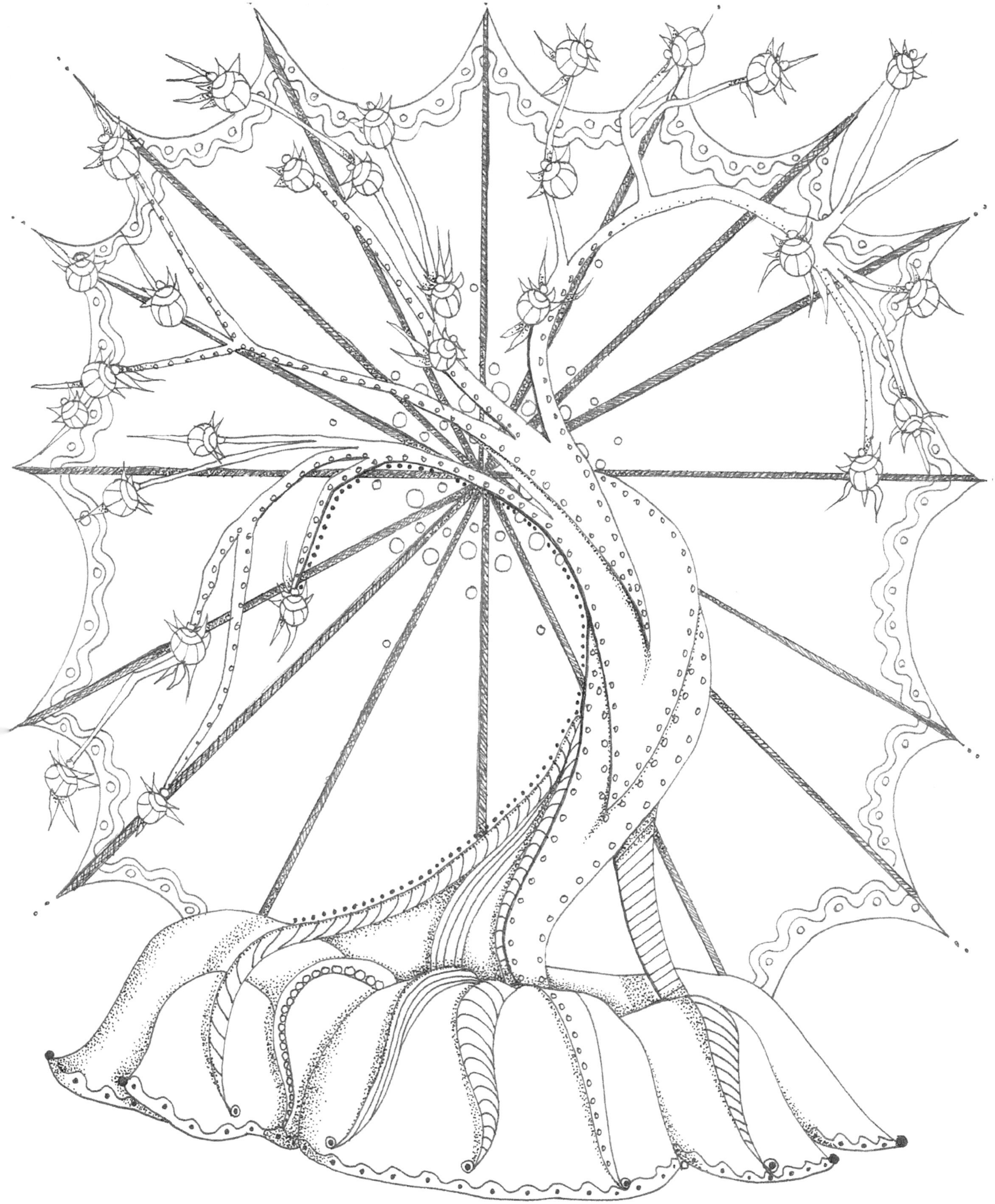

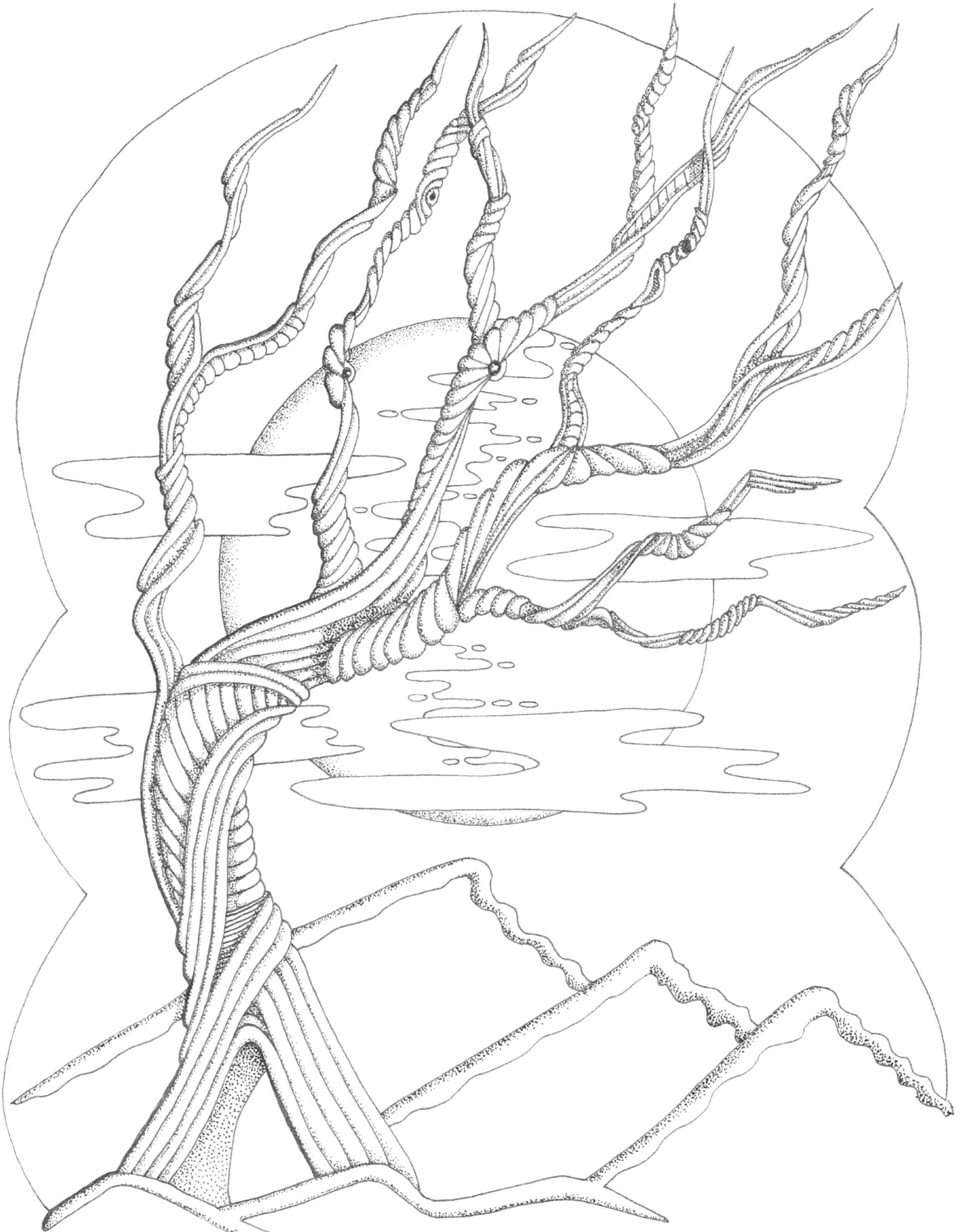

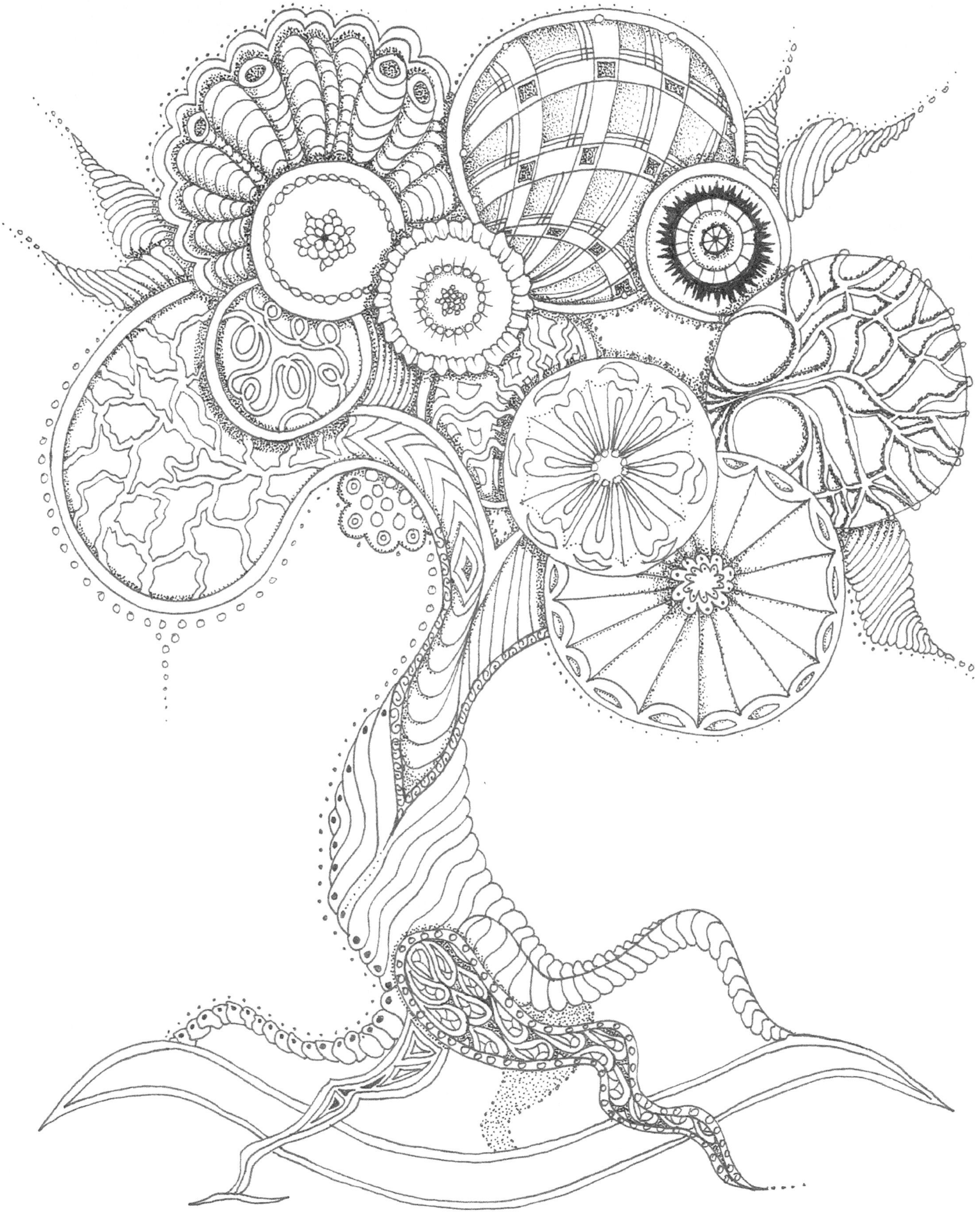

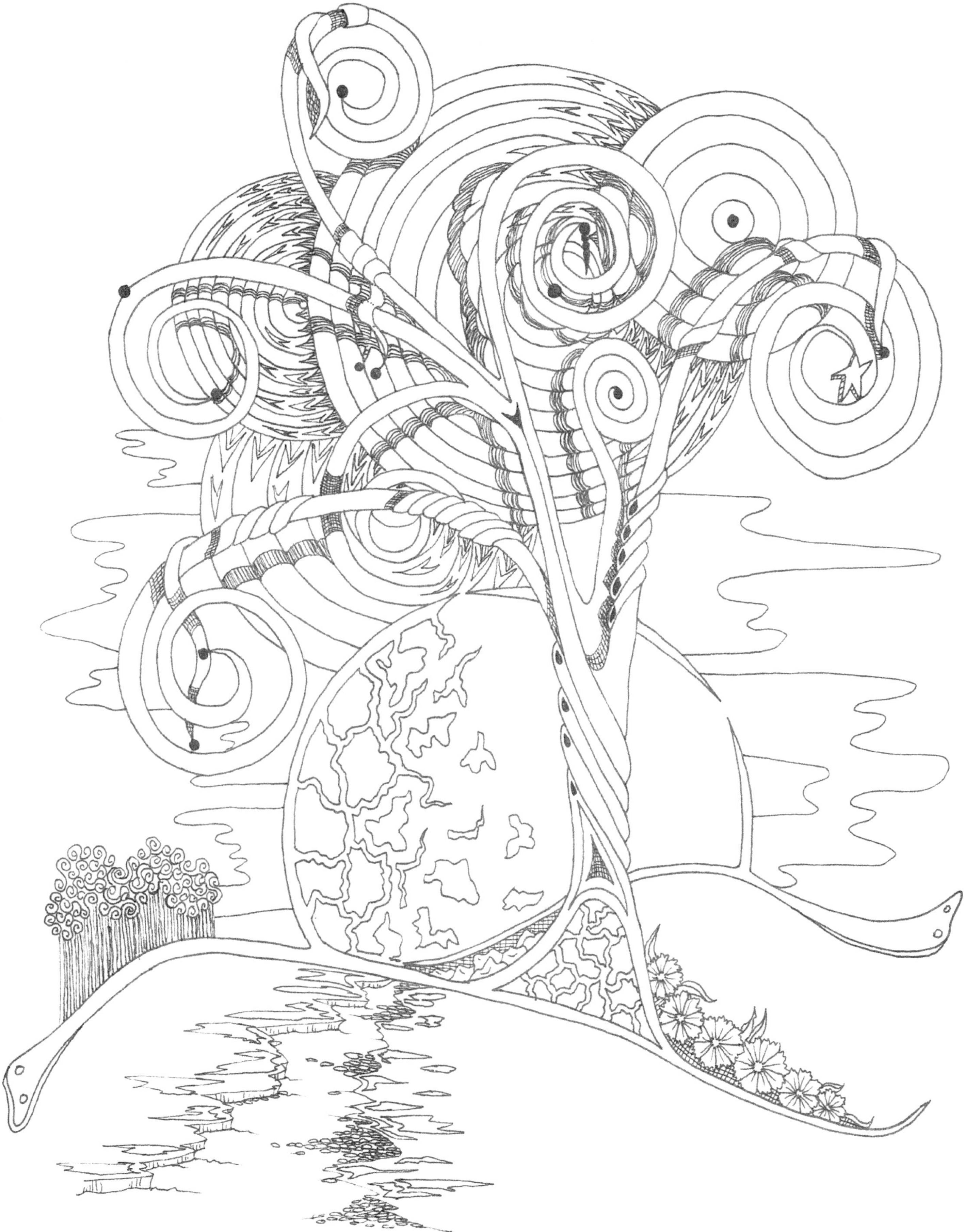

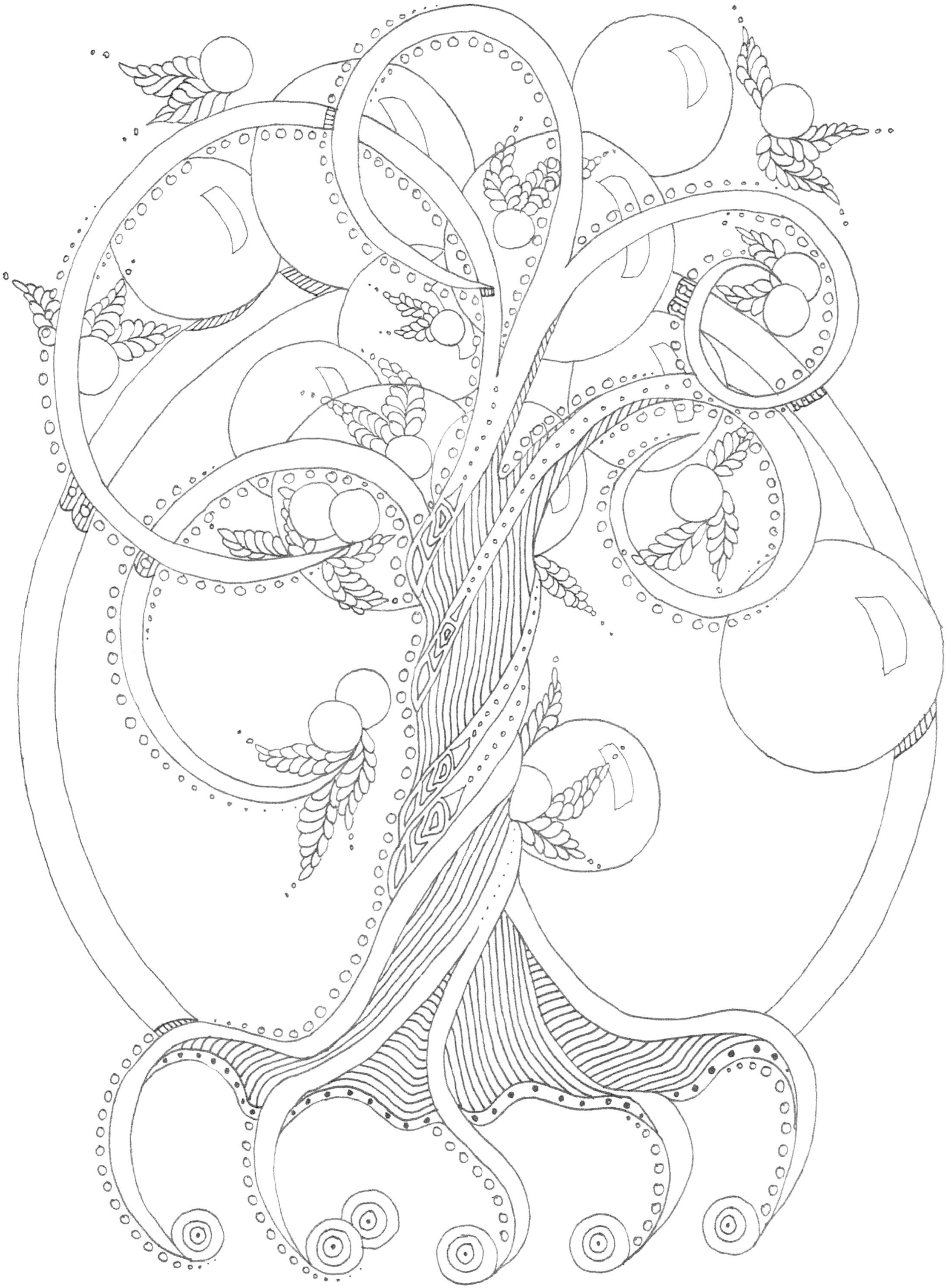

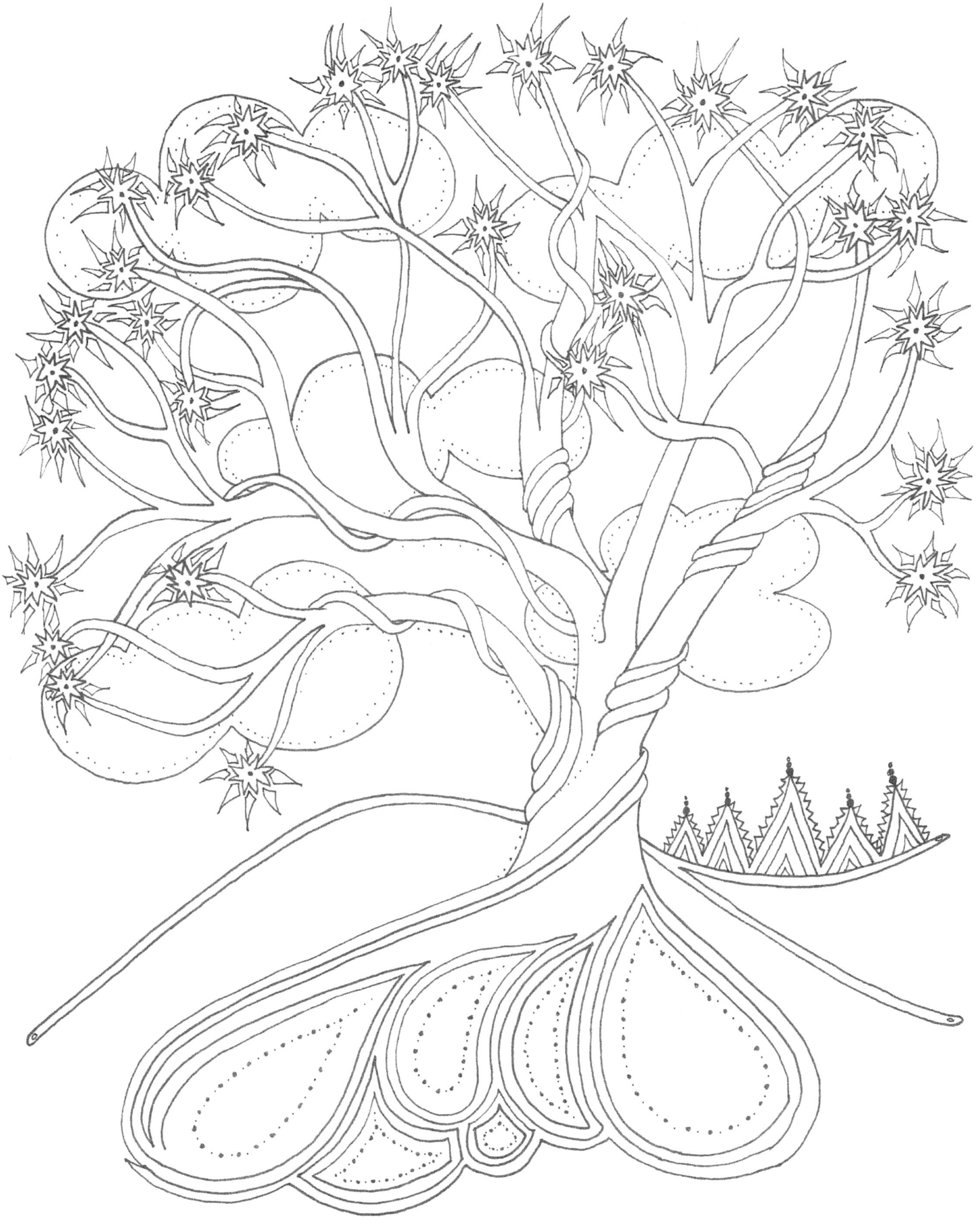

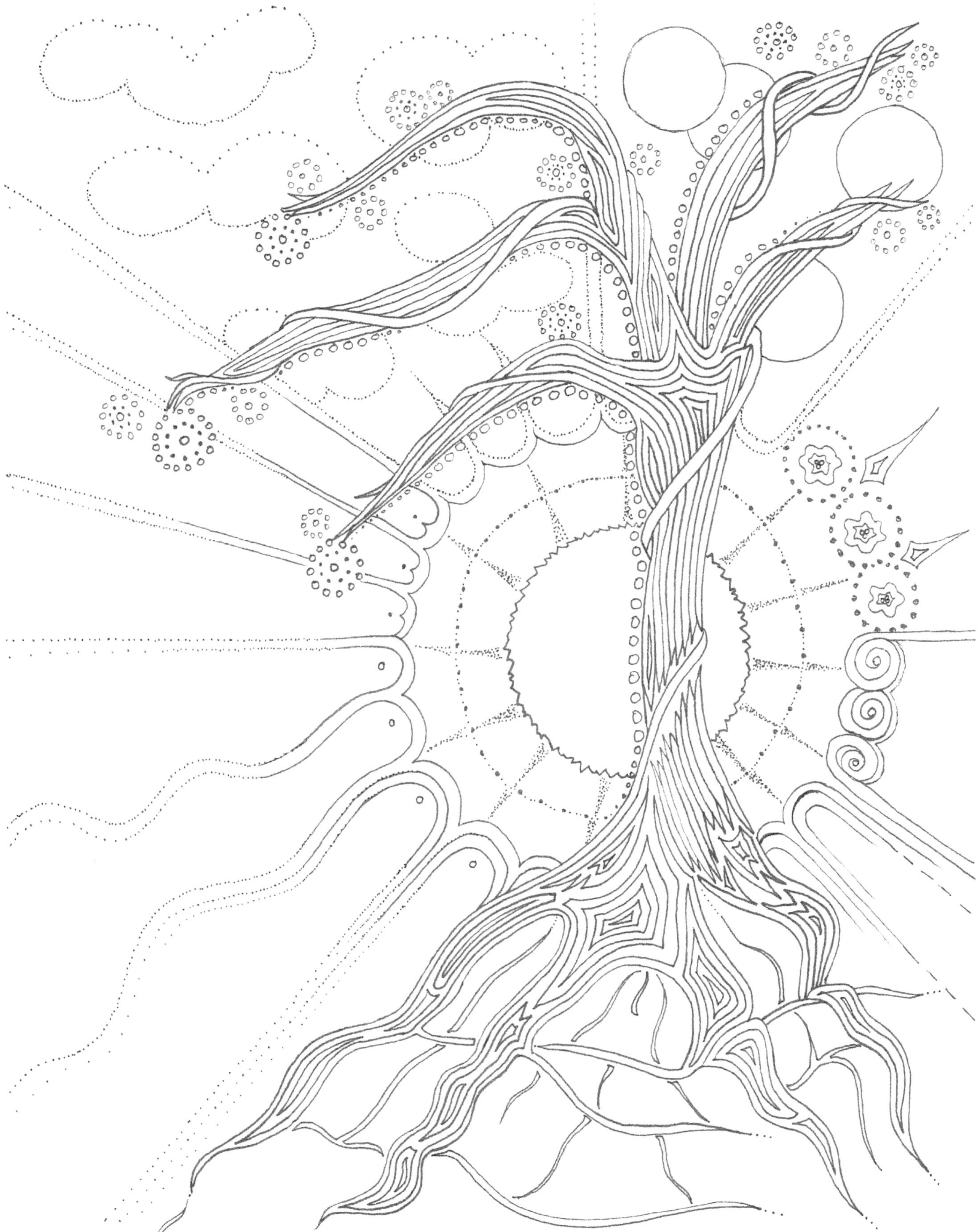

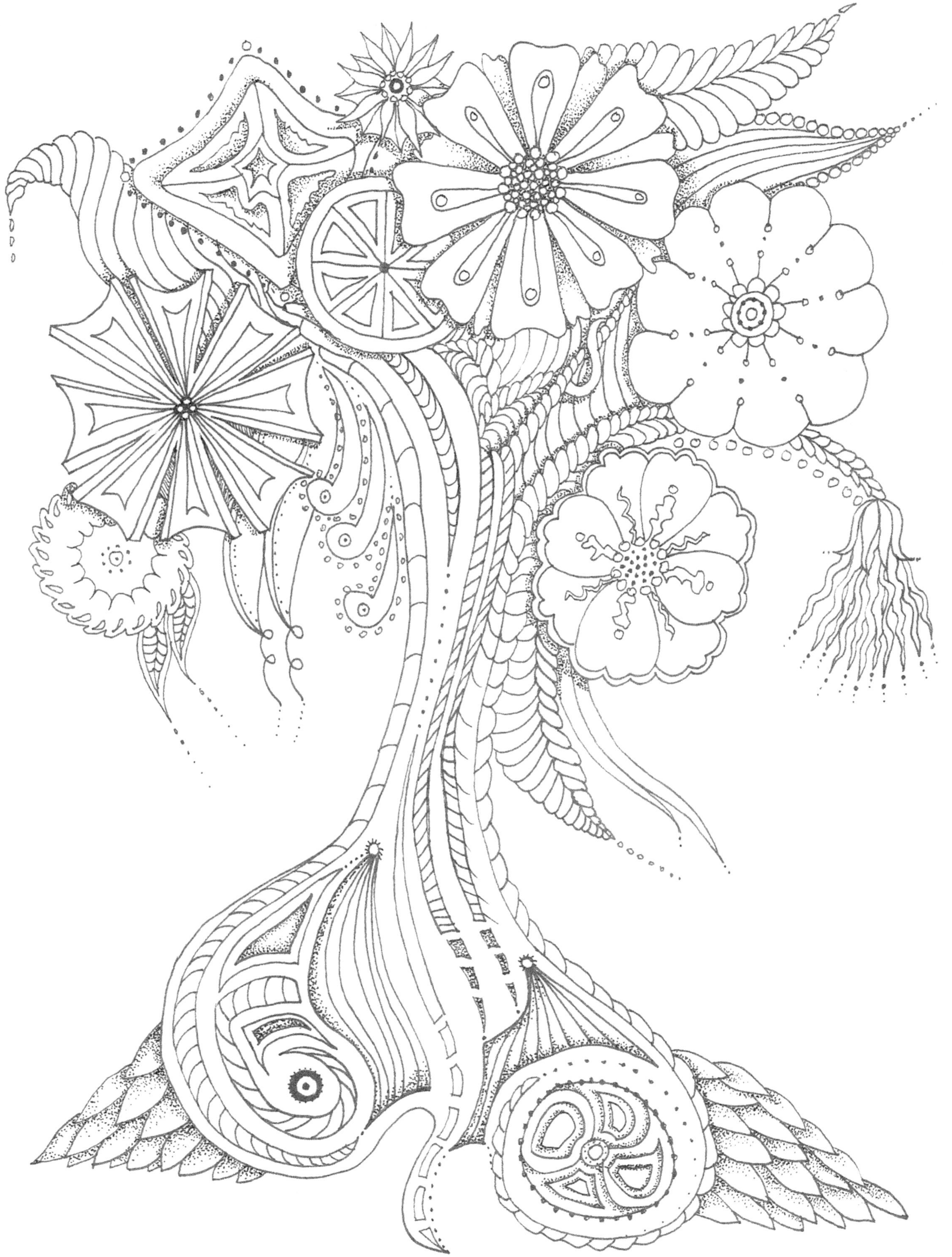

www.ingramcontent.com/pod-product-compliance
Lightning Source LLC
Chambersburg PA
CBHW080646190526
45169CB00009B/3521
* 9 7 8 1 5 3 0 7 9 3 5 6 3 *